Whispers *of* Wisdom

BEDTIME STORIES
FROM THE BIBLE

FREE
Book

Unlock Your Free Bonus Book!

As a heartfelt **thank you** for choosing our book, we're delighted to offer you a **FREE book.**

GET THE
AUDIOBOOK

Exclusively On Audible

Scan To Download

Table of Contents

Introduction

In the quiet twilight hours, when the world is hushed and still, stories come alive. These are the stories that have shaped generations, molded nations, and provided spiritual nourishment for countless souls over millennia. They are the narratives of ordinary men and women who walked through extraordinary times, who navigated challenges with fortitude and celebrated victories with humility. This book, "Whispers Of Wisdom: Bedtime stories from the bible," is a unique collection of those timeless tales.

This book is a journey into the heart of biblical wisdom, bringing the stories of the Bible alive in a new and compelling way. They are tales that transcend time and place, bearing universal truths that speak to each one of us, no matter our age or where we come from. These are stories that teach us about courage and kindness, about the meaning of friendship and the power of faith, about forgiveness, trust, and the boundless love of God.

From the young shepherd boy David, who defeated the giant Goliath, to the wisdom of King Solomon, from the loyalty of Ruth to the courage of Queen Esther, each story in this collection serves as a conduit of moral and spiritual truths. "Whispers Of Wisdom" takes you through Noah's big adventure, Daniel's miraculous friendship with lions, and the moving tale of the Prodigal Son. It shares the awe-inspiring stories of miraculous feedings and healings, and tales of unending love, such as the Parable of the Lost Coin.

Each story in this book aims to evoke reflection and contemplation, providing a deeper understanding of the powerful messages inherent in the scriptures. These are stories that can be shared at bedtime, kindling the light of faith, the joy of hope, and the warmth of love.

Through the magic of words, we invite you to create your own vivid images, to picture the grandeur of Noah's Ark, the courage in Daniel's eyes, or the surprise on Zacchaeus's face when Jesus calls him. This allows for a deeper, more personal connection to the tales, one that goes beyond the surface, reaching into the soul.

"Whispers Of Wisdom: Bedtime stories from the bible" is not just a collection of tales, it is a treasure chest of lessons for life, wrapped in the warm, soothing blanket of bedtime stories. As you read them, whispering words of wisdom into the night, you pass down the greatest legacy of all - the enduring stories of faith, hope, love, and humanity.

We hope this book finds a cherished place in your home, bringing you and your loved ones closer to the timeless wisdom of the Bible, and sparking conversations that echo with the profound lessons these stories have to offer.

So here we invite you, to step into the world of "Whispers Of Wisdom." The stories are ready to unfold, their characters waiting to share their lives, their wisdom echoing through the ages, speaking to the heart. So pull up the covers, get nestled in, and let the whispers of wisdom fill the night.

Lily's Adventure: A Shepherd's Unending Love

Once upon a time, in a green and peaceful valley, there lived a kind shepherd named David. David had a flock of a hundred sheep that he loved and cared for deeply. Every day, he would lead them to lush meadows and clear streams where they could graze and drink.

One sunny morning, as David counted his sheep, he noticed that one was missing. It was a little white lamb with curly wool named Lily. David became worried and couldn't bear the thought of Lily being alone and scared.

He left the other sheep safely in the meadow and set off on a journey to find Lily. He walked through winding paths, over rocky hills, and through dark forests, searching high and low. His heart was filled with hope and determination.

Finally, after a long search, David heard a faint "baa" coming from a steep cliff. He carefully climbed up and saw Lily, trapped on a small ledge. Lily was frightened, unable to find her way back down.

With gentle hands, David reached out and lifted Lily to safety. Lily's eyes sparkled with gratitude as she nestled back into the shepherd's loving arms. David rejoiced, knowing that his little lamb was safe and sound.

On the way back to the flock, David explained to Lily, "You see, Lily, you are just like the sheep in a story Jesus once told. He said that if a shepherd has a hundred sheep and one goes astray, he will leave the ninety-nine and go after the lost one until he finds it. Jesus loves and cares for each one of us, just like I love and care for you."

Lily's heart was filled with warmth and joy as she understood the deep love of her shepherd. From that day forward, Lily stayed close to David, never straying from his side.

In this story, we learn about the parable of the lost sheep, which Jesus shared to teach us about God's love and care for each and every one of us. Just as the shepherd searched for his lost sheep, God searches for us when we feel lost or stray from His path. No matter how small or insignificant we may feel, God's love is always there to guide and protect us. Remember, you are precious to God, and He will always be there to bring you back to safety and love.

Daniel and the Lions' Friendship

Once upon a time, in a land far away, there lived a wise and faithful man named Daniel. He loved God with all his heart and sought to follow His commandments every day. Daniel had a special gift for interpreting dreams, which made him highly respected in the kingdom.

One day, the king of the land, King Darius, appointed Daniel as one of his trusted advisors. This made the other advisors jealous, and they plotted against Daniel. They convinced King Darius to pass a law stating that anyone who prayed to any god or man other than the king would be thrown into a den of hungry lions.

Despite the new law, Daniel remained steadfast in his faith. Every day, he continued to pray to God, giving thanks and seeking guidance. When the jealous advisors discovered Daniel's continued devotion, they eagerly informed King Darius, who was deeply saddened by the turn of events.

Although the king admired Daniel, he felt bound by his own law and had no choice but to order Daniel to be thrown into the lions' den. As Daniel was lowered into the den, King

Darius said, "May your God, whom you faithfully serve, rescue you!"

Throughout the night, King Darius couldn't sleep. He worried about Daniel and his safety. At the break of dawn, he rushed to the lions' den, calling out anxiously, "Daniel, servant of the living God, has your God been able to save you?"

To his immense relief, King Darius heard a voice from within the den. It was Daniel, unharmed and filled with joy. "My king," Daniel said, "God sent His angel to shut the lions' mouths. They have not harmed me because I am innocent in His sight."

Overwhelmed with gratitude and awe, King Darius ordered Daniel to be lifted out of the den. He then declared a new law throughout the land, acknowledging the power and greatness of Daniel's God.

From that day forward, Daniel continued to serve as a trusted advisor to King Darius, and his faith and wisdom shone brightly. The lions in the den became his friends, for God had protected him and shown His mighty power.

In this story, we learn about the courage and faith of Daniel. Despite facing great danger, he remained faithful to God and continued to pray. God protected Daniel and showed His power by sending an angel to keep the lions from harming him. This story reminds us that when we trust in God and stay faithful, He can deliver us from any challenge or difficulty we face. Just like Daniel, we can find strength in our relationship with God and experience His miraculous interventions in our lives.

Noah's Big Adventure

Once upon a time, in a world filled with chaos and disobedience, there lived a righteous man named Noah. Noah loved God deeply and followed His commandments faithfully. One day, God spoke to Noah and revealed a plan to cleanse the earth with a great flood. God instructed Noah to build an ark and gather two of every kind of animal, along with his family.

Noah obeyed God's instructions without hesitation. He spent years building the massive ark, while people around him mocked and doubted. As the ark neared completion, Noah and his family diligently gathered the animals, taking them into the safety of the ark.

When the time came, rain poured from the heavens, and the earth was covered in water. Inside the ark, Noah and his family cared for the animals, ensuring their well-being throughout the flood. They trusted in God's promise to protect them and guide them to safety.

After forty days and forty nights, the rain ceased, and the floodwaters gradually receded. Noah sent out a dove to find dry land, and it returned with an olive leaf, a sign that the waters were receding. Eventually, the ark came to rest on a mountaintop.

Noah and his family joyfully stepped out of the ark, thanking God for His faithfulness. God made a covenant with Noah, promising never to destroy the earth with a flood again, symbolized by a rainbow in the sky.

Noah's obedience, faith, and perseverance in building the ark teach us the importance of following God's instructions, even when others doubt us. This story reminds us of God's faithfulness to His promises and His desire to protect those who are faithful to Him.

Noah's story reminds us that God keeps His promises. Just as He protected Noah and his family during the flood, God promises to be with us and take care of us in our own lives. We can trust in His faithfulness, even when things seem uncertain or challenging.

So, remember, just like Noah, be obedient, have faith in God, and trust that He is always watching over you, guiding you through any storm that comes your way. No matter what happens, God's love and faithfulness will be with you, just like it was with Noah and his family.

David and Goliath: The Little Shepherd's Triumph

In the land of Israel, there was a young shepherd boy named David. He was strong in spirit and had unwavering faith in God. One day, a giant warrior named Goliath challenged the Israelite army to send out their best soldier to fight him. Goliath's intimidating presence frightened the soldiers, and none of them dared to accept the challenge.

When David heard about Goliath's boastful challenge, he knew he had to act. David approached King Saul and offered to fight the giant. Despite David's young age and small stature, his faith in God gave him courage.

King Saul hesitated but eventually agreed. He dressed David in his own armor, but it was too heavy for the young shepherd. David decided to trust in God and faced Goliath with only a slingshot and five smooth stones.

As Goliath approached, mocking and taunting, David remained steadfast. He boldly declared, "You come against me with a sword and spear, but I come against you in the name of the Lord Almighty!" David swung his slingshot and launched a stone, which struck Goliath in the forehead. The giant fell to the ground, defeated.

The Israelites rejoiced, and David became a hero. His unwavering faith in God and his willingness to stand up against the seemingly insurmountable challenge of Goliath teach us that no obstacle is too great when we trust in God's strength.

This story inspires us to have faith in God's power, even when facing giants in our own lives. It teaches us that with God by our side, we can overcome any adversity and accomplish great things, regardless of our size or age.

In the story of David and Goliath, we learn that size and strength don't matter as much as faith and courage. David, a young shepherd boy, faced a giant warrior named Goliath. But instead of being afraid, David trusted in God's power and stepped forward to fight.

This story teaches us that we can conquer our fears and challenges when we have faith in God. No matter how big or scary the obstacles may seem, God is always with us, giving us the strength and courage to overcome them.

Just like David, you might face challenges in your life that seem too big to handle. But remember, with God on your side, you can face anything. Trust in Him, be brave, and never underestimate what you can achieve when you rely on God's strength.

So, when you face your own "giants" - whether it's a difficult task, a tough situation, or someone who doubts you

- remember that God is there to help you. Put your trust in Him, be brave, and know that He will guide you to victory.

Jonah and the Big Fish: A Lesson in Second Chances

Once upon a time, there lived a man named Jonah. God called Jonah to deliver a message to the people of a city called Nineveh. But Jonah was scared and didn't want to go, so he decided to run away from God's command.

Jonah boarded a ship heading in the opposite direction of Nineveh. However, God sent a powerful storm that rocked the ship and endangered everyone on board. Realizing that the storm was because of Jonah's disobedience, the sailors threw Jonah overboard to save the ship.

As Jonah sank into the depths of the sea, a giant fish swallowed him whole. Inside the fish's belly, Jonah cried out to God, repenting for his disobedience and asking for forgiveness. God heard Jonah's prayer and commanded the fish to spit him out onto dry land.

This time, Jonah listened to God's call and went to Nineveh. He warned the people of the impending judgment, and to his surprise, they listened and repented of their wrongdoings. God saw their change of heart and showed them mercy, sparing the city from destruction.

The story of Jonah and the Big Fish teaches us important lessons. It shows us that we cannot hide from God, and He always gives us second chances. Jonah learned that it's better to listen and obey God rather than trying to escape His plans.

For kids, this story reminds us that we should listen to our parents, teachers, and elders when they guide us in the right direction. It's essential to be obedient and responsible for our actions. If we make mistakes or choose the wrong path, we can always turn to God, ask for forgiveness, and He will give us a fresh start.

Remember, just like Jonah, God loves us and wants the best for us. He is always ready to forgive and give us another chance. So, be open to God's guidance, make wise choices, and trust that He will lead you on the right path.

The Wise King Solomon

Once upon a time, in the land of Israel, there was a king named Solomon. Solomon was known for his great wisdom, given to him by God. People from all over the world came to seek his counsel and hear his words of wisdom.

One day, two women came before King Solomon with a baby. They both claimed to be the baby's mother and argued fiercely, each insisting that the child belonged to her. King Solomon listened attentively to their passionate pleas.

In his wisdom, King Solomon devised a plan to determine who the real mother was. He ordered a sword to be brought and commanded, "Cut the baby in half, and each of you shall receive a half."

One of the women cried out in horror, "No, my lord! Please, let the baby live and give him to the other woman." But the other woman remained silent, agreeing with the king's judgment.

King Solomon immediately knew who the true mother was. He said, "Give the living child to the first woman. She is the real mother, for she would rather see her baby live than to have him divided." The people marveled at King Solomon's wisdom and fair judgment. They praised God for blessing their land with a wise and just king.

The story of King Solomon teaches us the value of wisdom and fairness. King Solomon's wise decision demonstrated his deep understanding of a mother's love. He knew that a true mother would do anything to protect her child, even if it meant letting go.

This story reminds us to seek wisdom in our own lives. When faced with difficult decisions or conflicts, it is important to consider the well-being of others and act with fairness and compassion. We should strive to find peaceful resolutions and show empathy for those around us.

Furthermore, the story highlights the importance of selflessness and sacrificing our own desires for the sake of others. Just like the true mother who was willing to give up her claim to the baby, we should prioritize love and care for one another.

So, let us remember the wisdom of King Solomon and aspire to be fair, compassionate, and selfless in our actions. Through wisdom and kindness, we can make the world a better place.

The Last Supper

Once upon a time in a faraway land, there lived a wise and kind man named Jesus. He traveled from town to town, spreading love, joy, and good teachings. One evening, as the sun dipped below the horizon, Jesus invited his closest friends, the twelve disciples, for a special supper.

The disciples were excited and gathered around a long wooden table. Jesus smiled warmly and said, "My dear friends, tonight is a special night. Let us share a meal together before I must leave."

As they sat together, Jesus took a loaf of bread, broke it into pieces, and passed it around. "Take and eat," He said, "this bread represents my body, which will be given for you."

The disciples were puzzled but followed His words. Next, Jesus took a cup of wine and passed it around. "This wine represents my blood, which will be shed for you," He said.

As they shared the meal, Jesus reminded them of the importance of love, forgiveness, and caring for one another. He knew that soon He would face difficult times, but He wanted His friends to remember these precious teachings.

One of the disciples, named Judas, felt troubled in his heart. He was tempted by greed and jealousy, and he made a terrible decision. He betrayed Jesus and revealed His whereabouts to those who sought to harm Him.

Jesus knew what was happening, but He did not respond with anger or hate. He continued to show love and compassion to everyone, including Judas. He forgave him for his actions, hoping that one day, Judas would find peace in his heart.

After the supper, Jesus and the disciples went to a garden to pray. He knew that His time on Earth was coming to an end, but He remained strong in His faith and trust in God. He asked His disciples to stay awake with Him, but they fell asleep, tired from their journey.

In the darkest hours of the night, soldiers came and arrested Jesus. He was taken away, and the disciples felt sad and afraid. They didn't understand why this was happening, but they held on to the lessons Jesus had taught them.

In the days that followed, Jesus faced great challenges and suffering. But through it all, He remained true to His teachings of love, forgiveness, and kindness.

The moral of this story is that love and forgiveness are powerful forces that can heal even the deepest wounds. Just like Jesus forgave Judas for his betrayal, we should also learn to forgive others when they make mistakes. By doing so, we can create a world filled with love, understanding, and compassion, making it a better place for everyone. So, before you go to sleep tonight, remember to forgive and love, just like Jesus did. Goodnight, dear child, and always remember the power of a forgiving heart.

Moses and the Burning Bush: A Call to Leadership

In the land of Egypt, the Israelites were enslaved by the Pharaoh. One day, a man named Moses, who had been raised as an Egyptian prince but was of Hebrew descent, was tending to his sheep near Mount Sinai.

As Moses guided his flock, he noticed a peculiar sight—a bush that was on fire but was not consumed by the flames. Curiosity filled his heart, and he approached the burning bush. To his astonishment, a voice called out from within the flames, saying, "Moses, Moses!"

Trembling with awe, Moses replied, "Here I am."

God spoke to Moses from the burning bush and revealed His divine plan. He instructed Moses to return to Egypt and demand the freedom of the Israelites from Pharaoh's oppression. Though Moses felt unworthy and unsure of his abilities, God assured him that He would be with him every step of the way.

With courage ignited in his heart, Moses obeyed God's command. He confronted Pharaoh, performed miraculous signs, and led the Israelites out of Egypt through the parted waters of the Red Sea. Despite facing numerous challenges and the doubts of his people, Moses remained steadfast in his faith and unwavering in his commitment to God's mission.

The story of Moses and the Burning Bush teaches us that God can use ordinary individuals to accomplish extraordinary things. It reminds us that even when we feel inadequate or afraid, God equips us with the strength and guidance we need to fulfill His purpose for our lives.

Through Moses' story, we learn the importance of listening to God's call, trusting in His power, and embracing the leadership roles He assigns to us. It encourages us to be brave, obedient, and to rely on God's strength, knowing that He is always present and will guide us through any challenges we may face.

The Miraculous Feeding of the Five Thousand

In the time of Jesus, great crowds followed Him wherever He went, eager to hear His teachings and witness His miracles. One day, as the sun began to set, a vast multitude had gathered in a remote place to listen to Jesus.

Seeing that the people were hungry and there was no nearby food, Jesus asked His disciples if they had any food to share. A young boy came forward with his small lunch—a meager offering of five loaves of bread and two fish.

Jesus took the boy's humble gift, looked up to heaven, and gave thanks. He then instructed His disciples to distribute the food among the crowd. Miraculously, the meager offering multiplied in Jesus' hands, and everyone present was fed. Not only did all the people eat, but there were also twelve baskets full of leftovers.

The feeding of the five thousand is a testament to Jesus' power and compassion. It teaches us the significance of offering what little we have and trusting in God's ability to multiply it beyond measure. This story reveals that when we offer our resources, no matter how insignificant they may seem, to Jesus, He can use them to bless others abundantly.

This story serves as a reminder of the importance of generosity and selflessness. It encourages us to share what we have, no matter how small, and trust in God's provision. It instills in us a belief that even their seemingly insignificant contributions can make a difference in the lives of others.

As we go about our day, we should look for opportunities to help those around us. It could be as simple as sharing a meal, giving a kind word, or lending a helping hand. In doing so, we too become a part of God's miraculous work in the world, spreading love and compassion just as Jesus did.

So as we close our eyes tonight and journey into the realm of dreams, may the story of the feeding of the five thousand fill our hearts with generosity, faith, gratitude, and trust. May it inspire us to share, to give thanks, and to trust in Jesus' care and providence. Good night, and may your dreams be filled with blessings multiplied.

David and Jonathan:
A True Friendship

In the kingdom of Israel, there was a young shepherd named David, who had a heart filled with love for God. He was brave and had defeated the giant Goliath, gaining the favor of King Saul. David's most cherished bond was with Jonathan, the son of King Saul.

David and Jonathan formed a deep friendship that was rooted in their shared faith and mutual respect. They supported and encouraged each other in times of triumph and difficulty. Jonathan recognized David's anointing as the future king and willingly surrendered his own right to the throne, affirming David's destiny.

Despite the challenges they faced, David and Jonathan remained loyal to one another. They made a covenant of friendship, promising to protect and care for each other's families. Their bond was unbreakable, and their friendship served as an example of love, trust, and selflessness.

The story of David and Jonathan teaches us the value of true friendship. It illustrates the importance of supporting and uplifting one another, even in the face of adversity. We learn that true friends stand by each other, celebrate each other's successes, and provide comfort and encouragement during challenging times.

This story also emphasizes the qualities of loyalty, sacrifice, and selflessness within a friendship. It teaches us to prioritize the well-being and happiness of their friends, just as David and Jonathan did.

Furthermore, the story encourages us to cultivate our relationships based on trust, respect, and shared values. It teaches us the importance of choosing friends who inspire us to be our best selves and who walk alongside us on our journey of faith.

So, let the story of David and Jonathan inspire us to cherish and nurture our friendships, and to strive to be loyal and supportive friends ourselves.

The Prodigal Son:
A Father's Unconditional Love

In a far-off place, a wealthy man lived with his two sons. Perhaps you can imagine the grandeur of their home, the fields stretching as far as your eyes can see, the laughter echoing through the halls. The younger son wanted to explore the world beyond the home he knew so well. He asked his father for his share of the inheritance, and with a heart heavy like a stone sinking into a river, his father agreed.

With a pocket full of gold and dreams, the younger son set off on his adventure. Can you picture him, standing at the crossroads, choosing his path? Unfortunately, his choices led him down a road of reckless living, and soon he was penniless and hungry. In his heart, a seed of regret started to grow. He decided to return home, ready to apologize, to ask for his father's forgiveness.

Now, think about how it would feel to see your home after a long time away. The young son was afraid, unsure of the welcome he might receive. Yet, something unbelievable happened. His father, upon seeing him from a distance, ran towards him. Can you imagine his surprise as his father wrapped him in a warm, welcoming embrace? His father's joy filled the air, a grand feast was arranged, and the house was filled with celebration.

But this story has another twist. The elder son, who was always loyal and obedient, like a rock amidst a stormy sea, couldn't understand his father's joy. He felt a surge of resentment, much like when you feel overlooked. His father, noticing this, pulled him close and explained the power of unconditional love. He urged his elder son to let go of his resentment and to rejoice in his brother's return.

Now, as you think about this story, remember the lessons it holds. Know that just like the father in the story, God's love for you is limitless. Even if you make mistakes or lose your way, God is always there to welcome you back with open arms. Remember that it is never too late to say sorry and to start again.

And don't forget about the elder son's lesson. Forgiveness and empathy towards others, even when it feels hard, are qualities to cherish. Celebrate when a lost one is found, a friend says sorry, or when a sibling shares a toy they didn't want to. Every day offers a chance to practice the joy of forgiveness and to cherish the love shared among us.

As you fall asleep tonight, carry these lessons in your heart. Remember the father's love, the joy of the return, and the elder son's lesson. Let these guide you as you dream under the starlit sky.

The Healing of the Blind Beggar: Faith and Compassion

In a town filled with people, noise, and life, there sat a blind beggar by the roadside. Can you imagine his world, like a night without stars, longing for the gift of sight? One day, a stir of excitement swept through the crowd. Jesus was passing by.

Upon hearing this, the blind beggar raised his voice, he cried out, "Jesus, Son of David, have mercy on me!" Even when people tried to quiet him, he persisted. He believed, deep down in his heart, that Jesus could grant him sight.

Jesus, hearing the man's cries, stopped. Picture the moment as Jesus called for him. With compassion that warms like a snug blanket on a chilly night, Jesus restored the man's sight. Can you imagine his joy, seeing the world's colors, shapes, and faces for the first time?

The man, now able to see, became a follower of Jesus. He praised God and shared his miraculous story far and wide.

As you think about this story, remember the lessons it teaches. Just like the blind beggar, never lose faith in God's power, even when others try to discourage you. Remember that persistence can lead to great things.

This story also shows the importance of being kind and compassionate to everyone you meet. Picture yourself in Jesus' shoes, reaching out with love and understanding. Remember to extend your own kindness to those in need, just like Jesus did.

And don't forget to appreciate the gifts you have. Every morning when you open your eyes to a new day, take a moment to be grateful for the ability to see the world around you. Use your gifts, whatever they may be, to make the world a better place.

So, as the night falls and you snuggle under your warm blankets, let this story fill your dreams. Let it inspire faith in God's power, a heart full of compassion, and gratitude for all your blessings. Good night, and may your dreams be as bright and hopeful as the morning sun.

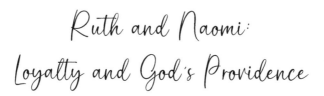

Ruth and Naomi: Loyalty and God's Providence

In the land of Bethlehem, there was a woman named Naomi, whose life had been marked by loss. With her husband and two sons gone, she was left alone like a solitary tree in an empty field. With a heart as heavy as a stone, Naomi made a decision to return to her homeland, like a bird flying back to its nest, hoping for a fresh start.

Her daughter-in-law, Ruth, was a beacon of love and loyalty in Naomi's life. Ruth vowed to Naomi, "Where you go, I will go. Where you stay, I will stay. Your people will be my people, and your God will be my God."

And so, they journeyed together to Bethlehem, overcoming the twists and turns of life with steadfast courage. In Bethlehem, Ruth was a hard worker, tirelessly gathering grain from the fields owned by Boaz, a man who was as generous as the sun is bright.

Boaz, touched by Ruth's unwavering loyalty and virtue, offered his protection and care. Over time, Boaz and Ruth married, their union a beautiful melody in the symphony of life, bringing joy and restoration.

As you listen to the tale of Ruth and Naomi, consider the lessons it offers. See the importance of loyalty and compassion, as Ruth chose to stand by Naomi in the face of adversity. Learn that God, like a master artist, often uses the broad strokes of hardship to paint a beautiful picture of blessings in our lives.

The story also serves as a reminder of the joy found in embracing diversity. Just as Ruth chose to love and respect Naomi's people and her God, you too can choose to accept and show kindness to those who may seem different from you. It underlines the importance of unity and shared values in a community.

As you prepare to sleep, let the story of Ruth and Naomi rest in your heart. May it bloom into a flower of loyalty, compassion, acceptance, and trust in God's plan for you. Good night, and may your dreams be filled with love and kindness.

The Fiery Furnace: Trusting God in Difficult Times

In the vast kingdom of Babylon, the powerful King Nebuchadnezzar ruled with an iron fist. The king, as proud as a peacock, built a magnificent golden statue. He commanded everyone, as numerous as the stars in the sky, to bow down and worship this golden figure.

But Shadrach, Meshach, and Abednego, three steadfast followers of God, stood tall like ancient oak trees in a forest, refusing to bow down to any idol. Their defiance sparked a fire of rage in King Nebuchadnezzar, who ordered these three friends to be thrown into a furnace that roared and crackled like a wild beast.

Even as they faced the fiery furnace, Shadrach, Meshach, and Abednego remained as calm as the surface of a tranquil lake, their faith in God unshaken. When they were cast into the flames, an astonishing sight revealed itself. Within the fiery dance, four figures were seen, moving unscathed, as though they were strolling in a gentle spring breeze.

King Nebuchadnezzar, his eyes as wide as the full moon, called them out of the furnace. They emerged, untouched by the devouring flames, a testament to the miraculous protection of God. Struck by this divine power, the king commanded that no one should speak against their God. He honored Shadrach, Meshach, and Abednego for their unwavering faith, as firm as a mountain against the storm.

Listen to this tale of Shadrach, Meshach, and Abednego, and reflect on the lessons it imparts. It shows the significance of holding onto your beliefs, even when winds of adversity try to shake you. It reminds you of the power of God's protection, a shield against the fiercest of trials.

May you learn from the steadfast faith of these three friends, and may it encourage you to trust in God's strength during times of tribulation. Be reminded of the importance of integrity, choosing to uphold your faith, even if it means standing against the crowd.

As you contemplate this story, let it be a guiding light, illuminating the path of trust in God, steadfast faith, and uncompromising integrity in your own journey. Good night, and may your dreams be filled with courage and peace.

The Good Samaritan: Compassion and Loving One's Neighbor

Once upon a time in the land of Israel, a man was journeying from Jerusalem to Jericho. Out of nowhere, he was ambushed by robbers, leaving him with nothing but his life, clinging onto it by the faintest thread. People passed by, including a priest and a Levite, who saw him but chose to walk on by as if he was an invisible ghost.

Then, imagine the surprise - a Samaritan, who was often judged and scorned by the Jewish community, saw the wounded man. He didn't walk past, instead, his heart filled with compassion like a bubbling spring. He cared for the man's injuries, lifted him onto his donkey as gently as a feather, and brought him to a nearby inn. There, the Samaritan promised to pay for any extra care the injured man might need, placing love and care above all else.

Jesus told this story as a lesson of love and kindness, asking, "Who, out of the priest, the Levite, and the Samaritan, was a neighbor to the man who was ambushed by robbers?" The answer was clear as day: "The one who showered him with kindness."

The tale of the Good Samaritan shines a light on the power of compassion and kindness, and the importance of extending a helping hand to those in need. It shows that being a neighbor doesn't rely on living next door but extends to everyone we meet.

Remember, your small acts of kindness can be like a ray of sunshine in someone's stormy day. This story urges you to lend your ears, your heart, and your hands to those who need it, regardless of who they are or where they come from.

And remember, this tale urges you to look beyond what you see. It encourages you to break away from preconceived notions and see everyone around you as worthy of kindness and respect.

So, let the tale of the Good Samaritan guide you on your journey. Be the one who shows kindness, the one who lends a hand, the one who is a true neighbor. May this tale inspire you to fill your heart with compassion and your days with acts of love. Good night, and may your dreams be filled with warmth and kindness.

The Unseen Heroes: A Story of Servanthood

In the heart of Galilee, a small village was nestled among the hills. Here, a family named Jacob, Sarah, and their two children, Levi and Miriam, lived. Jacob was a gifted carpenter, and Sarah, with all her heart, cared for their cozy home.

One day, the village was buzzing with excitement. Can you guess why? Yes, Jesus, the well-known teacher and healer, was passing through their village! Everyone was eager to see Him and learn from His wisdom.

Amidst the hustle and bustle, Jacob and Sarah saw a golden chance to serve Jesus. They didn't have heaps of gold or vast lands, but what they did have was a warm home. They decided to welcome Jesus and His disciples into their home for some rest and a hearty meal.

With joy bubbling in their hearts, they prepared a meal full of love and care. They cleaned their home until it sparkled, and waited for Jesus with open hearts. As Jesus and His disciples stepped into their home, they welcomed them with wide smiles, offering a space of warmth and nourishment.

As they shared the meal, Jacob and Sarah listened to Jesus' words like eager learners, taking in every drop of wisdom. They watched as Jesus healed the sick and comforted the sorrowful, all while sharing God's message of love.

Jacob and Sarah didn't perform miracles or preach powerful sermons like Jesus. Yet, their simple act of service provided a backdrop of love and care, supporting Jesus' mission. Their humble hospitality created a safe haven for Jesus and His disciples, a place to rest and regain strength.

When it was time for Jesus to leave, He looked at Jacob and Sarah, His eyes full of gratitude. He said, "Know this, anything you've done for the least of these, you've done for Me."

This tale of The Unseen Heroes shows you the power of humble service and the magic of small acts of kindness. It's a reminder that everyone has a special part to play in the world, no matter who they are or what they have.

Remember, serving others with a humble heart is like a beautiful song of love and faith. Look for chances to spread warmth, help those in need, and create an environment full of love and acceptance.

This tale shows that even the smallest acts of kindness can make a big difference and be part of the great work in the world. You too can be an unseen hero, touching lives with your acts of kindness and compassion.

So, let the tale of The Unseen Heroes inspire you to serve with love, to cherish the power of small acts of kindness, and to use your unique gifts to serve others. Good night, may your dreams be filled with love and kindness.

The Lost Coin: The Value of Every Soul

Let's visit a bustling city, where a kind and generous woman named Rebecca lived. She owned ten shiny silver coins, each one a treasure to her.

One day, as Rebecca was carefully counting her coins, she found out that one was missing! She searched in every nook and cranny of her house, turning everything upside down, but the coin was still missing. Not giving up, she lit a lamp and swept the entire house, because she was determined to find her precious coin.

Can you imagine how hard Rebecca must have looked for that coin? After hours of searching, she finally spotted a little sparkle underneath a dusty corner. Feeling excited, she bent down and found her lost coin. She was so happy that she invited all her friends and neighbors to celebrate with her.

As everyone gathered around, Rebecca shared her story. She said, "Just like this coin was lost and now is found, each of us holds great value in the eyes of God." This reminds us of the story Jesus shared about the lost sheep. Jesus said that even if one sheep was lost, the shepherd would leave the ninety-nine and go searching until he finds it. And when he finds it, he would celebrate with joy.

Just like the lost coin and the lost sheep, each one of you is very important and precious to God. No matter if you feel lost or insignificant sometimes, always remember that God's love for you is limitless.

You, too, are cherished by God, even if you think you have flaws or make mistakes. This story hopes to encourage you to see the worth and dignity in yourself and in others around you.

It's also a call for you to show kindness and reach out to those who may feel lost or forgotten. Just like Rebecca did for her lost coin, or the shepherd did for his lost sheep, you can extend a helping hand, offering love and support to those who need it most.

The Lost Coin is a gentle reminder of how special each of you are, and of the importance of looking out for those who might feel lost. I hope it inspires you to be a shining light of love, compassion, and acceptance in a world where everyone deserves to be valued and cherished.

The Mustard Seed:
Faith's Mighty Growth

Once upon a time, in a cozy little village, there was a young girl named Anna. Anna loved hearing stories about Jesus and His teachings from her mom and dad. One sunny day, she asked her dad, "How can tiny things make a big difference?"

Her father's eyes sparkled, and he said, "Let me share with you the amazing story of the mustard seed."

Long, long ago, Jesus explained to His friends about the strength of faith. He told them, "Even if your faith is as tiny as a mustard seed, you can tell a mountain to move, and it will! Nothing will be too difficult for you."

Anna's eyes grew wide, wondering how this could be possible. She set off on an adventure to discover the secret of the mustard seed. Finding a teeny, tiny mustard seed, she marveled at how it could hide such a big secret.

Feeling excited, Anna decided to plant the mustard seed in a patch of earth. Each day, she cared for it, watering it gently, and waited for something magical to happen. Days turned into weeks, and weeks turned into months, and Anna watched and waited with hope in her heart.

One bright morning, Anna awoke to an incredible sight. The small mustard seed had grown into a towering tree, its branches reaching out like welcoming arms. Birds had made their homes in it, chirping merrily in the morning sun.

Her heart filled with joy, Anna understood the wonderful secret of the mustard seed. It wasn't about how small the seed was, but the amazing potential it held inside. Just like the mustard seed, even a small amount of faith could grow into something extraordinary.

Anna couldn't wait to share her discovery! She told everyone, "Even if we feel small, with faith in God, we can do amazing things!"

The Mustard Seed story is a lesson for all of you about the power of faith. It wants to encourage you to believe in something bigger than yourselves. Even when things seem hard or doubtful, keep your faith strong, like a little mustard seed.

You can make a big difference, no matter how small you think you are. This story teaches you to believe in yourself and know that, with faith and God's help, you can do wonderful things.

Also, recognize your own potential and the potential in others. You can nurture your dreams, grow your talents, and trust that God can turn small beginnings into extraordinary things.

The Mustard Seed story hopes to remind you that your faith can move mountains. I hope it inspires you to believe in all the wonderful things that are within you. Remember, even the smallest acts of faith can grow into something truly magnificent!

The Persistent Widow: Trusting in God's Justice

In a place not too far away, nestled between green meadows and tall trees, a town hummed with life. There lived a brave widowed woman named Rachel, who had a heart full of courage and faith. But one day, a new ruler came to the town, who didn't play fair, making things hard for everyone.

Rachel saw this and it made her very sad. She decided that she had to do something about it. So she walked straight up to the ruler's grand castle and knocked on his huge door. She asked him nicely to be kind and fair to everyone. But the ruler, with his mind full of selfish thoughts, didn't listen to her words.

But you know what? Rachel didn't let this stop her! She put on her bravest face and went back to the ruler every single day, asking him again and again to do the right thing. The ruler was becoming tired of her daily visits but still, he didn't change his ways. But Rachel, with a heart filled with hope and eyes sparkling with determination, didn't give up. She believed with all her heart that God saw everything and would help make things right.

Finally, after many days, the ruler saw the fire of faith in Rachel and decided to listen to her. Rachel's brave heart and never-give-up spirit had made him see that it was important to be fair and kind to everyone.

Now, listen closely, my little ones. This story of the Persistent Widow, of brave Rachel, shows us how important it is to always stand up for what is right. Even when things seem tough, don't ever give up! Know that your voice is important and can make a big difference.

And always remember, just like Rachel, when you put your trust in God and always seek to do what's right, He will be there to guide and help you. So, as you snuggle into your beds tonight, think about brave Rachel and remember, always be kind, be fair, and never ever give up!

The Talents:
Using Gifts to Multiply Blessings

Once upon a time, in a town buzzing with the noise of busy shops and markets, lived a clever man named Samuel. He knew how to make a good deal better than anyone else! One day, Samuel called his three trusted helpers and gave each of them a bag of shiny, golden coins.

To the first helper, he gave five bags full of gold coins. To the second one, he gave two bags, and to the last one, he gave a single bag. Samuel gave them a special mission, "Use these gold coins wisely and make them grow while I am away on a journey."

Now, the first helper was as eager as a beaver! He got to work immediately, using the gold coins to buy things that he could sell for more money. And guess what? He was able to turn his five bags of gold coins into ten!

The second helper saw this and thought, "I can do that too!" So he put his coins to work and carefully bought and sold things until he had turned his two bags into four.

But the third helper, he was as scared as a mouse. He thought he might lose the coins, so he decided to bury the one bag of gold coins he had, deep in the ground.

When Samuel came back, he asked his helpers how they had done. The first two helpers were as happy as larks! They showed Samuel all the extra gold coins they had earned. Samuel was so pleased, he said, "Well done! You used what I gave you and made it grow. Now, I trust you to take care of even more things!"

But when the third helper came forward, he only had the same single bag of gold coins. He told Samuel that he was too scared to try and make it grow. Samuel was disappointed and said, "You could have at least put my money in the bank to earn a little bit more."

Now my little ones, this story, the story of The Talents, wants to tell you something very special. It wants to tell you that each one of you is given a wonderful gift by God. It could be the gift of drawing beautiful pictures, telling fantastic stories, making people laugh, or even being a good friend.

Just like the helpers with the bags of gold coins, you have to use these gifts and make them grow. Don't be like the third helper who was too scared to use what he had. Be brave! Use your gifts to make the world around you a better place.

As you close your eyes tonight, remember, God has given you something special. Don't be afraid to use it. Be like the first and second helpers and watch as your talents bless the world!

Esther's Courageous Stand: A Young Queen's Brave Decision

Once upon a time, in the land of Persia, there was a sweet and lovely girl named Esther. She lived with her kind cousin Mordecai, who cared for her like she was his very own daughter. Esther was not only very beautiful but also kind and gentle-hearted.

Now, one day, the king of Persia, King Xerxes, decided he needed a new queen. So, a royal order was given to find the most beautiful and charming girls in the kingdom, and Esther was chosen to go to the palace.

Guess what happened next, my dear ones? The king met Esther, and he thought she was the most wonderful girl he had ever seen. He chose her to be the queen! But in the palace, there was a mean man named Haman who did not like Esther's people and wanted to harm them.

When Mordecai found out about Haman's nasty plan, he sent a message to Esther. He asked her to use her new position as queen to help her people. But approaching the king without being invited could be very dangerous, even for the queen, and Esther was scared.

Mordecai told Esther something very wise. He said, "Esther, maybe you became the queen just so you could help us at a time like this." Esther felt a stirring in her heart. She knew Mordecai was right.

With all the courage she could muster, Esther made a plan. She hosted a big feast for the king and Haman. In the middle of the feast, she bravely told the king about Haman's evil plan. The king was so angry at Haman that he decided to punish him!

Because of Esther's bravery, her people were saved from a terrible fate. The king made a new law allowing them to protect themselves. Mordecai was honored, and there was a grand celebration!

The story of Esther, my dear ones, is a reminder of how brave and courageous we can be, even when we're scared. Just like Esther, we can stand up for what is right and make a big difference in the world. As you snuggle up in your beds tonight, remember that you, too, can be brave and stand up for others. Let the story of brave Queen Esther guide you in your dreams tonight.

Joshua and the Battle of Jericho: A Mighty Conquest by Faith

In a land filled with towering mountains and lush green valleys, there lived a courageous leader named Joshua. He was strong and brave, with eyes that sparkled like the stars in the night sky. Joshua was chosen by God to lead the Israelites, a special group of people, into a new land called Canaan.

One day, the Israelites came to the city of Jericho. It was a grand city with walls that stretched high into the sky. The people of Jericho were strong and fierce, and they did not want the Israelites to enter their city.

But Joshua had faith in God's plan. He gathered the Israelite army and shared God's instructions. They were to march around the city once a day for six days, with seven priests carrying trumpets made of shining gold. On the seventh day, they were to march around the city seven times, and when Joshua gave the signal, the priests were to blow their trumpets and the people were to shout with all their might.

With hope in their hearts, the Israelites followed Joshua's command. They marched around Jericho, their footsteps creating a rhythmic beat. The priests blew their trumpets, the sound resonating through the air. But the walls of Jericho remained standing.

On the seventh day, the Israelites woke up filled with anticipation. They marched around the city as Joshua had instructed. As they completed the seventh lap, Joshua raised his hand and shouted, "Shout, for the Lord has given us the city!"

The Israelites let out a mighty cheer. They shouted with all their might, and something incredible happened. The walls of Jericho started to shake and crumble. Dust filled the air as the walls came tumbling down, making way for the Israelites to enter the city.

With hearts full of joy, the Israelites rushed into Jericho. They celebrated their victory and thanked God for His mighty power. They knew that it was because of their faith and trust in God that the walls had fallen.

Joshua and the Israelites learned an important lesson that day. They learned that with faith and obedience, anything is possible. They saw firsthand the power of God's love and how He can make the impossible possible.

Children, as you close your eyes and drift off to sleep, remember the story of Joshua and the Battle of Jericho. Let it fill you with hope and faith. Just like Joshua and the Israelites, remember that with God by your side, you can conquer any challenge that comes your way. Trust in His plan and have faith in His love, and you will see amazing things happen.

Goodnight, and may your dreams be filled with courage and adventure.

Mary and Martha: Balancing Hospitality and Devotion

In a quaint village nestled amidst rolling hills, there lived two sisters named Mary and Martha. Mary had eyes that shone with curiosity and a heart eager to learn, while Martha possessed a warm smile and a natural talent for caring for others. They both loved Jesus dearly and cherished His teachings.

One day, Jesus and His disciples came to visit Mary and Martha's home. Excitement filled the air as the sisters prepared for their special guests. Martha, filled with a desire to serve, bustled about the kitchen, preparing a feast fit for a king. She wanted everything to be perfect for Jesus and His followers.

Meanwhile, Mary sat at the feet of Jesus, listening intently to His every word. She was captivated by His wisdom and filled with a deep sense of peace in His presence. Her heart was focused solely on learning from her beloved teacher.

As the preparations continued, Martha began to feel overwhelmed by all the work. She grew frustrated and noticed that Mary was not helping. In her frustration, Martha approached Jesus and said, "Lord, don't you care that my sister has left me to do all the work alone? Tell her to help me."

Jesus looked at Martha with eyes filled with love and understanding. He gently replied, "Martha, Martha, you are worried and upset about many things, but few things are needed—or indeed only one. Mary has chosen what is better, and it will not be taken away from her."

Martha's heart softened as she realized the truth in Jesus' words. She understood that while serving and hospitality were important, it was equally crucial to set aside time to be with Jesus, to listen to His teachings and draw close to Him.

From that day forward, Mary and Martha learned to strike a balance between their love for hospitality and their devotion to Jesus. They discovered that true worship went beyond serving and encompassed opening their hearts to His presence and growing in their understanding of His teachings.

As you lay your heads upon your pillows, remember the story of Mary and Martha. Let it remind you of the importance of finding balance in your lives. Just like Mary, take time to listen and learn from Jesus, and like Martha, let your love for others shine through acts of kindness and hospitality. May you find joy in serving others while keeping your hearts open to the love and wisdom of our Savior. Goodnight, and may your dreams be filled with blessings.

Joseph and the Coat of Many Colors: Dreams and Forgiveness

In a land adorned with vibrant tapestries of colors and blossoming fields, there lived a young boy named Joseph. Joseph had a heart filled with dreams, and his eyes shimmered with hope and wonder. He was the favorite son of his father Jacob, who gifted him a magnificent coat of many colors.

Joseph's dreams were like windows to another world. One night, he dreamt of sheaves of wheat bowing down to him. Excitedly, he shared his dream with his brothers. But instead of celebrating his dreams, they grew jealous and plotted against him.

Filled with envy, Joseph's brothers decided to take away his coat and sell him as a slave to a passing caravan. They tore the colorful garment from him, leaving Joseph in tattered clothes and a heart filled with sadness.

Joseph was taken far away to a foreign land called Egypt. There, he became a servant in the house of a wealthy man named Potiphar. Despite the hardships he faced, Joseph held onto his dreams and remained faithful to God

One day, a terrible lie was told about Joseph, and he was thrown into prison. But even in the darkest of places, Joseph's faith never wavered. He used his God-given gift of interpreting dreams to bring hope to those around him, including two fellow prisoners.

Years passed, and Joseph's reputation as a dream interpreter reached the ears of the mighty Pharaoh. Summoned to the palace, Joseph listened as Pharaoh recounted his puzzling dream of cows and grain. Guided by God's wisdom, Joseph revealed that the dream was a warning of a coming famine

Impressed by Joseph's wisdom, Pharaoh appointed him as a high-ranking official. Joseph was given the task of preparing Egypt for the impending famine. He stored grain and provisions, ensuring that the people would have enough to eat during the difficult times ahead.

Back in Joseph's homeland, the famine also struck, affecting his family. Joseph's brothers, unaware of his fate, traveled to Egypt seeking food. When they stood before Joseph, they did not recognize him. Overwhelmed with emotion, Joseph revealed his true identity, and tears flowed as they embraced.

Instead of seeking revenge, Joseph chose forgiveness. He saw that his brothers had changed, regretful for their past actions. With a heart full of compassion, Joseph forgave them and welcomed his family to live in Egypt, reuniting with his father Jacob.

The story of Joseph teaches us about the power of forgiveness and the fulfillment of dreams. It reminds us that even in times of adversity, holding onto our faith and remaining true to our values can lead to incredible blessings.

As you drift off to sleep, remember Joseph's story. Let it inspire you to hold onto your dreams, even in challenging times, and to embrace forgiveness and compassion. May your dreams be filled with hope, and may you awaken with a heart ready to forgive and embrace the colorful tapestry of life. Goodnight, and may your dreams be filled with joy.

Elijah and the Ravens: A Lesson in Divine Provision

Once upon a time, in the sun-baked lands of Israel, there lived a humble and devoted man named Elijah. He was not just any man; he was a prophet, chosen by God to deliver messages to the people.

One day, God spoke to Elijah, warning him about a severe drought that would grip the land. "Go east," God instructed him, "hide by the Kerith Brook, east of the Jordan. You will drink from the brook, and I have ordered the ravens to feed you there."

Elijah was surprised. Ravens? These black-feathered creatures were scavengers, known more for their cawing and their love of shiny things. But Elijah trusted in God's word and set off east, towards the brook.

Upon reaching his destination, he found a quiet spot by the Kerith Brook. As the sun started to set, painting the sky with hues of red and orange, he heard a familiar cawing sound.

And then he saw them. Two sleek, black ravens swooped down from the sky, each carrying something in their beaks. As they neared, he saw that they were holding bread and meat. They landed softly near him, offering their cargo.

With a heart full of gratitude, Elijah ate his unexpected meal, marveling at God's creativity in providing for him. And as the days turned into weeks, the ravens kept visiting Elijah every morning and every evening, each time bringing him food.

Even when the brook began to shrink due to the drought, the divine provision through the ravens never ceased. This extraordinary experience taught Elijah a powerful lesson about God's resourcefulness and care, a lesson that would resonate through generations.

So, as you drift into sleep tonight, remember the story of Elijah and the ravens. Recall the trust Elijah placed in God's wisdom and care, despite his dire circumstances. With faith like his, you can rest assured, knowing that God's provision is always within reach. Sweet dreams, and may they be filled with the fluttering wings of providence.

Deborah:
The Courageous Judge and Warrior

Once upon a time, in the time of the Israelites, a land where rolling hills met endless skies, there lived an exceptional woman named Deborah. She was known throughout the lands for her wisdom and courage. She was not only a prophetess, receiving divine visions, but also a judge, settling disputes and offering wise counsel to her people.

In this era, the Israelites were living under the oppressive rule of King Jabin of Canaan, and his ruthless army commander, Sisera. Sisera commanded a formidable army with 900 iron chariots, striking fear in the hearts of the Israelites. The people were downtrodden, their spirits low, and they cried out for help.

God heard their pleas and, in a vision, gave Deborah a plan for deliverance. She saw the Israelites, led by a brave man named Barak, facing Sisera's mighty army and emerging victorious. This divine guidance filled her with a determined resolve.

Calling for Barak, she shared God's plan, "The Lord, the God of Israel, commands you: 'Go, take with you ten thousand men and lead them up to Mount Tabor. There, I will lure Sisera, the commander of Jabin's army, with his chariots and troops to you, and I will deliver him into your hands.'"

Barak, though a brave warrior, hesitated at the enormity of the task. "If you go with me, I will go," he proposed, seeking the comfort of Deborah's wise presence. "But if you don't go with me, I won't go." Deborah agreed to accompany him but warned, "Because of this decision, the honor of defeating Sisera will not be yours. God will hand Sisera over to a woman."

And so, with Deborah's presence bolstering their confidence, Barak and his ten thousand men marched against Sisera's intimidating forces. The ground shook as they clashed on the battlefield, the roar of the conflict echoing in the hills. Despite their fear, the Israelites held onto their faith, remembering Deborah's prophecy of their victory.

The battle was fierce, and slowly, against all odds, the tide began to turn in favor of the Israelites. But Sisera, seeing his forces diminishing, fled from the battlefield.

True to Deborah's prophecy, Sisera's end came not at the hands of a man but a woman. He sought refuge in the tent of a woman named Jael, who seized the opportunity to end the tyrant's reign and became the unexpected hero of the story.

Deborah's story, filled with wisdom, courage, and divine guidance, serves as a beacon across generations. It teaches us that faith can yield unexpected victories, and no matter how formidable the opposition, deliverance is possible.

As you settle into sleep tonight, remember Deborah, the prophetess, the judge, and the warrior. Let her story fill your dreams, reminding you that with faith, courage, and wisdom, you can overcome any challenges that stand in your way. Good night, and may your dreams be as bold and as brave as Deborah's spirit.

The Conversion of Saul: A Story of Transformation and Mercy

In a time long ago, a man named Saul walked the dusty roads of Damascus. Saul was no ordinary man; he was a Pharisee, zealous in his faith and feared by many. His reputation was known far and wide, for he relentlessly persecuted those who followed Jesus, the man who claimed to be the Messiah.

One day, as Saul journeyed to Damascus, a brilliant light from heaven suddenly engulfed him. He fell to the ground and heard a voice speaking to him, "Saul, Saul, why do you persecute me?"

Stunned and confused, Saul asked, "Who are you, Lord?

"I am Jesus, whom you are persecuting," the voice replied. "Now get up and go into the city, and you will be told what you must do."

Blinded by the intense light, Saul was led by his companions into Damascus. For three days, he was without sight, neither eating nor drinking.

In the city lived a devoted disciple named Ananias. God spoke to him in a vision, "Go to the house of Judas on Straight Street and ask for a man from Tarsus named Saul, for he is praying. In a vision, he has seen a man named Ananias come and place his hands on him to restore his sight.

Despite his fear of Saul's reputation, Ananias trusted God's command. He went to the house and found Saul. Placing his hands on Saul, Ananias said, "Brother Saul, the Lord—Jesus, who appeared to you on the road as you were coming here—has sent me so that you may see again and be filled with the Holy Spirit."

Instantly, something like scales fell from Saul's eyes, and he could see again. Filled with the Holy Spirit, Saul was baptized, and he began to preach about Jesus in the synagogues, proclaiming that He is indeed the Son of God. The people were amazed and asked, "Isn't this the man who caused such devastation among Jesus' followers in Jerusalem?"

Saul, now also known as Paul, became one of the most passionate apostles of Christ. His life, a testament to the power of divine mercy and transformation, reminds us that no one is beyond the reach of God's grace.

As you lay down tonight, let the story of Saul's transformation seep into your dreams. Remember, it's never too late for change, and the light of divine love can touch and transform even the hardest hearts. May your sleep be peaceful, and your dreams be filled with the promise of new beginnings, just as Saul found on the road to Damascus.

The Story of Lydia: A Tale of Faith and Generosity

In the ancient city of Philippi, nestled by the eastern coast of the Aegean Sea, there lived a woman named Lydia. Her story begins in the bustling markets of the city, where vendors called out to passersby, their voices mingling with the rustle of leaves and the clatter of carts.

Lydia was no ordinary woman. She was a merchant who traded in purple cloth, a luxury item that was highly prized among the wealthy and the nobles. The deep, rich color was produced from the secretions of a tiny sea snail, making it a rare and valuable commodity. Lydia's skill in her trade had earned her a successful business and the respect of many.

However, Lydia was admired for more than her business skills. She had a reputation for her generous spirit and a heart that was kind and compassionate. When she walked through the markets, people would smile and wave, their eyes lighting up in her presence.

One day, new visitors arrived in Philippi. They were a group of men led by the apostle Paul, who was on a mission to spread the teachings of Jesus Christ. As was their custom, they sought a synagogue to share their message. But in Philippi, they found none. Undeterred, they ventured outside the city gates to the river, where they heard people gathered for prayer.

As they approached the river, they found a group of women who had come for prayer. Lydia was among them. The women listened attentively as Paul spoke of Jesus, His teachings, His crucifixion, and His resurrection. Lydia, with her open heart, found herself deeply moved by his words. A sense of peace washed over her, a feeling as refreshing as the river's cool water on a hot summer day.

When Paul offered baptism to those who believed in Jesus Christ, Lydia did not hesitate. She and her entire household were baptized, a symbol of their new faith and dedication to the teachings of Jesus.

Lydia, moved by the kindness of Paul and his companions, extended an invitation to them. "If you consider me a believer in the Lord," she said, her voice filled with the warm sincerity, "come and stay at my house." They accepted her gracious offer, and Lydia's home became a place of fellowship and support for the apostles during their time in Philippi.

Lydia's story serves as a shining example of how faith can touch and transform a person's life. Her generosity did not end at the doors of her home; it extended to her newfound spiritual family, supporting them in their divine mission.

Tonight, as you close your eyes and drift into sleep, remember Lydia. She was a successful merchant, a generous friend, a faithful believer. May her story inspire you to keep an open heart, ready to receive faith, and to extend a generous hand to those around you. May you dream of vibrant purple cloths and the warmth of shared faith, and wake refreshed, ready to face a new day.

Elijah and the Widow: A Story of Trust and Divine Providence

Many ages ago, in the land of Israel, there lived a prophet named Elijah. He was a man of unwavering faith who spoke God's words to the people and performed many miracles in God's name

During a particularly harsh time, there was a great drought throughout the land. The skies remained clear, with no sign of rain, and the fields grew parched under the blazing sun. In those difficult times, God instructed Elijah to leave Israel and journey to Zarephath, a small town in the region of Sidon.

Elijah, trusting in God's guidance, journeyed to Zarephath. As he approached the city gates, he saw a woman gathering sticks. God revealed to him that she was a widow and that he was to ask her for food and water.

But this was a time of great scarcity, and the widow herself was struggling to provide for her and her son. Upon hearing Elijah's request, she shared her plight. "As surely as the Lord your God lives," she said, "I don't have any bread—only a handful of flour in a jar and a little olive oil in a jug. I am gathering a few sticks to take home and make a meal for myself and my son, that we may eat it—and die."

Moved by her despair, Elijah assured her not to fear and made a promise. "Don't be afraid," he said. "Go home and do as you have said. But first make a small loaf of bread for me from what you have and bring it to me, and then make something for yourself and your son. For this is what the Lord, the God of Israel, says: 'The jar of flour will not be used up and the jug of oil will not run dry until the day the Lord sends rain on the land.'"

In an act of profound faith, the widow did as Elijah had asked. And true to Elijah's words, her jar of flour and jug of oil remained miraculously replenished, providing for her, her son, and Elijah throughout the duration of the drought.

The story of Elijah and the widow of Zarephath serves as a powerful reminder of God's providence and the blessings that can come from trust and generosity, even in the face of scarcity.

As you close your eyes to rest tonight, hold this tale close to your heart. Let the story of the widow's faith, Elijah's promise, and the unending jar of flour and jug of oil fill your dreams. May it remind you that even in the most challenging times, divine provision is never far away. Good night, and may your dreams be as plentiful as the widow's jar of flour.

Peter's Great Catch: A Tale of Faith and Calling

In the cool, early morning on the Sea of Galilee, a fisherman named Simon, who would later be known as Peter, was washing his nets on the shore. His clothes were damp, and his spirit was low. All night, he and his companions had been out on the water, and their nets remained stubbornly empty. It was one of those hard days when the sea refused to share its bounty.

As he washed his nets, a crowd gathered on the shore. Among them was Jesus of Nazareth, the man whose words had begun to stir hearts and minds across the region. Jesus asked Simon if He could use his boat as a platform to address the growing crowd. Simon agreed, and Jesus spoke from the boat, His voice carrying over the water to the eager crowd on the shore.

When He finished speaking, Jesus turned to Simon and told him, "Put out into deep water, and let down the nets for a catch."

Simon was taken aback. They had been fishing all night without any luck. However, something in Jesus' gaze stirred him. Despite his doubts, he said, "Master, we've worked hard all night and haven't caught anything. But because you say so, I will let down the nets."

With a deep breath, Simon directed the boat into deeper water. He let down the nets, the cords slipping through his fingers, and waited. Suddenly, the nets began to tug and thrash. Simon and his companions pulled the nets back into the boat, revealing an astonishingly large amount of fish, so many that their nets began to break. They signaled to their partners in the other boat to come and help them. They filled both boats, so much so that they began to sink.

Simon fell at Jesus' knees, awestruck and overwhelmed. Jesus comforted him, saying, "Don't be afraid; from now on you will fish for people."

From that day forward, Simon, now Peter, left his nets and followed Jesus, becoming one of His most devoted disciples. His faith and dedication would become an enduring inspiration for many generations to come.

Tonight, as the shadows of the day give way to the moon's soft glow, let the story of Peter's great catch echo in your dreams. Remember the miraculous load of fish, the breaking nets, and the boats near sinking. But most of all, remember Simon's trust in Jesus' words and his call to a higher purpose. May it inspire you to embrace faith and trust in your life's journey. Sleep peacefully, and may your dreams be as abundant as Peter's catch.

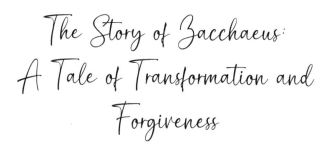

The Story of Zacchaeus: A Tale of Transformation and Forgiveness

In the ancient city of Jericho, there lived a man named Zacchaeus. Zacchaeus was a tax collector, a position that was not well-liked by the people as tax collectors often demanded more than required and kept the excess for themselves. Despite his wealth, Zacchaeus was lonely, and his heart yearned for something more than the riches he had amassed.

One day, a buzz of excitement filled the air. Jesus of Nazareth was coming to Jericho. Curiosity piqued, Zacchaeus decided to see this man he had heard so much about. However, because he was a short man and the crowd was large, he couldn't see past the throng of people.

Determined not to let this opportunity pass, Zacchaeus ran ahead of the crowd and climbed a sycamore tree to get a better view. As Jesus walked by, He looked up and, to Zacchaeus' surprise, spoke directly to him. "Zacchaeus," He called, "come down immediately. I must stay at your house today."

Joy surged through Zacchaeus as he scurried down the tree and welcomed Jesus gladly. However, the crowd murmured disapprovingly, for they could not comprehend why Jesus would choose to stay with a sinner like Zacchaeus.

In response to their disapproval, Zacchaeus stood and made a solemn vow. "Look, Lord! Here and now I give half of my possessions to the poor, and if I have cheated anybody out of anything, I will pay back four times the amount."

Jesus smiled at Zacchaeus, his promise signaling a transformation of heart. "Today, salvation has come to this house," Jesus declared. "For the Son of Man came to seek and to save the lost."

Zacchaeus' life changed forever that day. His wealth no longer defined him; instead, his transformed heart and redeemed actions did. He became known as a man of generosity and fairness, a testament to the power of grace and the possibility of change.

As you close your eyes tonight, let Zacchaeus' story echo in your dreams. Picture him perched in the sycamore tree, his eyes wide with anticipation, and then feel his joy when Jesus calls his name. May his story remind you that transformation is possible for everyone, and forgiveness is a gift to be received with joy. May you sleep peacefully, knowing that no matter how far one strays, one can always find a way back. Good night, and may your dreams be as joyful as Zacchaeus' transformation.

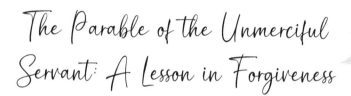

The Parable of the Unmerciful Servant: A Lesson in Forgiveness

In the ancient city of Jerusalem, Jesus taught His followers through parables, simple stories filled with profound wisdom. One of these was the Parable of the Unmerciful Servant, a tale that highlights the importance of forgiveness.

The story begins with a king who wished to settle accounts with his servants. Among them was one servant who owed him ten thousand bags of gold, a debt so enormous it was impossible for the servant to repay.

Unable to settle his debt, the king ordered that the servant, along with his wife, children, and all he had, be sold to repay the debt. The servant fell to his knees before the king, pleading for patience. "Be patient with me," he begged, "and I will pay back everything."

Seeing the servant's distress, the king took pity on him. He forgave the servant's debt, allowing him to go free. The servant left the king's presence, his heart filled with relief and gratitude.

However, this servant encountered a fellow servant who owed him a hundred silver coins, a much smaller amount. Grabbing him by the neck, he demanded, "Pay back what you owe me!" Despite the second servant's pleas for patience, the first servant had him thrown into prison until he could pay back his debt.

When the other servants saw what had happened, they were greatly distressed. They went and reported everything to the king. The king called the first servant back and said, "You wicked servant! I canceled all your debt because you begged me to. Shouldn't you have had mercy on your fellow servant just as I had on you?" In anger, the king handed him over to the jailers until he should pay back all he owed.

This parable, shared by Jesus, serves as a stark reminder of the importance of forgiveness. If we have been shown mercy, we must extend it to others, not hold onto grudges or demand retribution.

Tonight, as you drift into sleep, let the Parable of the Unmerciful Servant be a lullaby to your soul. Envision the scenes, the pleading servant, the forgiving king, and the unforgiven fellow servant. May it remind you to be merciful and forgiving, as you have received mercy and forgiveness. Sleep soundly, and may your dreams be filled with lessons of kindness and compassion. Good night, and may your rest be as peaceful as a forgiving heart.

Samson's Strength: The Power of a Promise

In a time long past, in the vibrant lands of ancient Israel, there was a man of remarkable strength named Samson. His story starts even before he was born, in the quiet life of a couple who lived in the town of Zorah.

This couple had been unable to have children, but their lives took a turn when an angel of the Lord appeared to them. The angel brought a message of hope, telling them they would have a son. But this would be no ordinary child. This son was to be a Nazirite, set apart for God, and he was destined to deliver Israel from their enemies, the Philistines.

As part of his Nazirite vow, there were certain rules he was to follow. He was to refrain from drinking wine, avoid contact with the dead, and most importantly, never cut his hair. It was in this uncut hair that his extraordinary strength resided, a symbol of his commitment to God.

Samson grew into a man of extraordinary strength. There were tales of him tearing a lion apart with his bare hands and slaying an entire army with just the jawbone of a donkey. His feats of strength were legendary, and the Philistines feared him.

Yet, Samson had a weakness - his love for a Philistine woman named Delilah. The Philistine rulers, eager to defeat Samson, coerced Delilah into discovering the secret of his strength. After much persuasion, Samson finally revealed his secret to Delilah: his uncut hair, the symbol of his vow to God, was the source of his power.

In his sleep, Delilah had his hair cut off. Samson woke up, thinking he could fend off any enemy as before, but his strength had left him. He was captured by the Philistines, who blinded him and made him grind grain in prison. But they overlooked one thing - hair grows back. As Samson's hair grew, so did his strength.

In the final act of his life, during a grand spectacle where he was brought forth to entertain the Philistine rulers, Samson prayed to God for strength one last time. He positioned himself between the two main pillars of the temple. With a mighty push, he brought down the pillars, causing the temple to collapse, killing himself and his captors.

Samson's story is a tale of mighty strength, but also one of the power of promises. His strength was a gift tied to his vow to God, showing us the importance of our commitments. As you rest your head and journey into the world of dreams tonight, reflect on the power of keeping promises. May your sleep be as peaceful as a promise kept, and your dreams be filled with the strength of integrity.

The Tower of Babel: A Lesson in Pride and Humility

In the sprawling plains of Shinar, nestled between the rivers of ancient Mesopotamia, there once thrived a civilization of men who all spoke the same language. There, in the cradle of civilization, they resolved to make a name for themselves that would echo through the ages.

They came up with an ambitious plan. Together, they would construct a grand tower reaching the heavens, a testament to their collective ingenuity and power. Using bricks for stone and tar for mortar, they set to work, their hearts swelling with pride.

Days turned into weeks, weeks into months, as the tower grew. Its imposing silhouette stood stark against the sky, growing higher and higher, a tangible symbol of human ambition and hubris. The builders dreamt of reaching the heavens, challenging the very limits set by God Himself.

Yet God, in His wisdom, saw what the people were doing. He knew their pride had led them astray, their ambition unmoored from humility. In response, He confounded their language, causing them to speak different tongues. Suddenly, the once unified builders could not understand each other. The communication that was the bedrock of their monumental project crumbled, and with it, their tower.

Unable to cooperate, the people scattered across the face of the earth, leaving behind the unfinished Tower of Babel - a testament to the dangers of unchecked pride. The once united people now found themselves in different lands, speaking different languages, a humbling reminder of their mortal limitations.

The story of the Tower of Babel teaches us a valuable lesson about pride and humility. While ambition is a powerful drive, it must be balanced with humility, acknowledging our human limitations and respecting divine boundaries.

As you close your eyes and prepare for a journey into the realm of dreams, remember the Tower of Babel. Imagine the towering structure, the confusion of languages, and the scattering of people. Consider the value of humility, even in our grandest plans. Let these lessons accompany you into your dreams, and may you wake with a renewed sense of balance and respect for the world. Sleep peacefully and wake refreshed, ready to build your dreams on the solid foundation of humility and respect.

The Donkey's Message: Balaam's Surprising Teacher

Once upon a time, in the land of Pethor, lived a man named Balaam. He was known far and wide as a prophet who could bless and curse through the power of his words. One day, the Moabite King Balak sent messengers to Balaam with a request to curse the Israelites, who were approaching his territory.

God appeared to Balaam and told him not to curse the Israelites because they were blessed. Balaam obeyed and sent the messengers back to King Balak. However, when the king sent more prestigious envoys with promises of great rewards, Balaam was tempted and set off towards Moab, even though God had told him not to go.

Balaam saddled his faithful donkey and began his journey. As they were traveling, an angel of the Lord, sword in hand, stood in their path, visible only to the donkey. Fearful, the donkey turned away, causing Balaam to strike her for straying off the path. This happened twice more, with the donkey seeing the angel and Balaam beating her for her supposed disobedience.

On the third occasion, in an incredible turn of events, the donkey spoke to Balaam. "What have I done to you," she asked, "that you have struck me these three times?" Balaam, surprisingly unphased by the talking donkey, replied that she had made a fool of him, and if he had a sword, he would kill her.

At this moment, God opened Balaam's eyes, and he saw the angel of the Lord standing in the road, sword drawn. The angel informed Balaam that if the donkey had not turned away, Balaam would have been killed. Balaam realized his mistake and confessed his sin, offering to return home. But the angel told him to proceed, instructing him to speak only the words God would give him.

The story of Balaam and his donkey teaches us that wisdom can come from the most unexpected places. Balaam, a prophet, learned an important lesson from his donkey about obedience to God and the dangers of greed and pride.

As you settle into your bed, let your thoughts drift to the ancient lands and the surprising tale of a donkey that saw an angel and spoke words of wisdom. Let this be a reminder that wisdom can come from unexpected places, and the importance of humility and obedience. As you journey into the world of dreams, may these lessons guide you. Sleep peacefully, and may your dreams be filled with wisdom and discovery.

www.ingramcontent.com/pod-product-compliance
Lightning Source LLC
Chambersburg PA
CBHW061709210125
20608CB00056B/1506